Dedication

To each child.
You are wonderful
just the way
you are.

Acknowledgments

I wish to thank Meredith Johnson, whose charming illustrations resonate so well with the text, and Marieka Heinlen for the exuberant design. I appreciate Judy Galbraith and the entire Free Spirit family for their dedicated support of the series. I am especially grateful to Margie Lisovskis for her diplomatic style as well as her talented editing. I also recognize Mary Jane Weiss, Ph.D., for her expertise and gift in teaching social skills. Lastly, I thank my fantastic family—David, Kara, Erika, James, Daniel, Julia, and Andrea—who are each an inspiration to me.

"Children and adults will love these gentle, empowering books. The Learning to Get Along series is a powerful tool for teaching children essential social skills such as empathy, respect, cooperation, and kindness. This straightforward and insightful series helps children visualize how their appropriate behavior positively impacts themselves and others. I heartily recommend this as a solid, classic resource for teaching affective skills to young children."

—Dr. Stephen R. Covey, Author, *The 7 Habits of Highly Effective People*

Accept and Value Each Person

Cheri J. Meiners, M.Ed.

Illustrated by Meredith Johnson

free spirit
PUBLISHING®

Library of Congress Cataloging-in-Publication Data
Meiners, Cheri J., 1957–
    Accept and value each person / by Cheri J. Meiners.
       p. cm.
    ISBN-13: 978-1-57542-203-9
    ISBN-10: 1-57542-203-4
1. Toleration—Juvenile literature. 2. Individual differences—Juvenile literature. I. Title.
    HM1271.M396 2006
    179'.9—dc22
                                                                                                    2005033708

Reading Level Grades 1–2; Interest Level Ages 4–8; Fountas & Pinnell Guided Reading Level H

Cover and interior design by Marieka Heinlen
Edited by Marjorie Lisovskis

10 9 8 7 6 5
Printed in Hong Kong
P17201110

Free Spirit Publishing Inc.
217 Fifth Avenue North, Suite 200
Minneapolis, MN 55401-1299
(612) 338-2068
help4kids@freespirit.com
www.freespirit.com

Each person in this world
is different from everyone else.

I'm the only one just like me.

There are many ways to tell us apart
on the outside.

We each have our own size, shape, and color that is just right.

But on the inside,
I'm a lot like other people.

I want people to like me just the way I am.

I want to know that I'm important
to someone.

Everyone wants to feel accepted.

I can like people for who they are,
and treat them kindly.

I can include another person.

There's room in my heart
for someone new.

I like to make friends.

I can listen and talk
to find ways that we're alike.

I have lots of friends.

Each one is interesting in a different way.

I can value the way each person looks, thinks, and feels.

We're each good at different things.

Sometimes I can help somebody.

At other times, someone can help me.

We all like different things.

We think, believe,
and do different things, too.

We may have differences in our families.

We may speak, eat, or dress
in different ways.

I can appreciate people just the way they are.

I may not like everything a person does.

I can be patient with others
when something bothers me.

When big problems happen,
I can listen as we talk about
our differences.

I can try to understand how someone feels.

I can forgive when I feel hurt.

I can respect and learn from each person I meet.

There's something I can like about everyone.

We're each an important part of a group.

We can do more together than alone.

When we accept and value each other,

we're learning to get along.

Ways to Reinforce the Ideas in
Accept and Value Each Person

As you read each page spread, ask children:

- What's happening in this picture?

Here are additional questions you might discuss:

Pages 1–3

- What is something about you that's different from everyone else? *(Besides physical differences, discuss distinctive attributes such as how individual children write or draw, specific skills or abilities, and things they think about.)*

- How do the different kinds of fish remind you of differences in people?

Pages 4–7

- How are people alike on the inside?

- Who are you important to? How do you know?

- What does it mean to feel accepted? *(You might explain acceptance as a feeling of belonging or of being okay just the way you are.)*

Pages 8–13

- Think of a time you made friends with someone new. How did you show that you wanted to be friends? How did you feel? How did the other person feel?

- How are the shells alike? How are they different? What if all the shells in the ocean were exactly alike?

- Think of a friend. How are you and your friend alike? How are you different? What do you like about your friend?

- What does *value* mean? *(You might explain by saying, "If you value something about someone, you appreciate it and think it's important.")*

Pages 14–15

- What is something you're good at? What are some ways you can help someone else? How does it feel to help?

- What are some things other people have done to help you? How does it feel when someone helps you?

Pages 16–19

- How are the people in this picture alike? How are they different? What different things are they doing?

- What's a family? How are families alike? How are they different?

- What are some ways people speak (eat, dress) differently?

- What if everybody looked alike? What if everybody wanted to do the same things?

Pages 20–25

- Tell about a time when you talked and listened during a disagreement with someone. How did you solve it?

- Why is it important to understand how someone else feels? How does this help us get along?

- What does it mean to forgive? *(You might explain by saying, "When you forgive someone, you decide not to feel hurt or bothered by what the person said or did.")* Have you ever forgiven someone? What happened? How did you feel after you forgave the person? Has someone ever forgiven you? What happened? How did you feel?

Pages 26–31

- What is respect? *(You might explain by saying, "When you respect people, you show that you think they are important.")* What are some ways you can show respect for someone?

- What are some of the groups you belong to? What are things that are easier to do in a group than alone?

"Appreciating Others" Games

Accept and Value Each Person teaches children about understanding and appreciating both the similarities and differences of others. The book introduces beginning skills of valuing and accepting others, showing kindness and respect, and learning to get along with others in our diverse society. Here is a summary of ten skills of accepting and valuing others that are taught in the book:

1. Treat everyone kindly.
2. Find ways you're alike.
3. Include someone who is new.
4. Learn to give and receive help.
5. Appreciate others the way they are.
6. Overlook small differences.
7. Talk and listen when differences cause a problem.
8. Try to understand how others feel.
9. Forgive when you feel hurt.
10. Value each person as part of the group.

Read this book often with your child or group of children. Once children are familiar with the book, refer to it when teachable moments arise involving positive behavior or problems related to accepting and valuing others. Notice and comment when children show kindness and compassion. In addition, use the activities on pages 34–35 to reinforce children's understanding of why and how to be accepting and respectful toward all people.

"Alike and Different" Game

Preparation: Prepare a worksheet with a grid of four to eight squares. In each square, write a topic or question like the following; photocopy a worksheet for each child.

- What is your favorite color (book, toy, school subject, game)?
- How old are you?
- How many teeth have you lost?
- How many people are in your family?

Directions: Read aloud a question from the worksheet, and have or help children fill in their answer using words or simple pictures. Continue until all squares are filled. Then go over the questions and answers as a group. Talk about the ways children are alike and different.

Variation: After children have completed the worksheets, give each child a blue and red crayon. Have children form groups of two or three to compare how they answered the questions. Ask children to tally on their worksheets their group members' responses to the questions: If another child answered the same way, the child will put a blue X in the box, and a red X if the answer is different. Then have children compare their findings of how many ways they are similar or unique in the group. Have children think of a few ways they are all the same.

"Valuing New Friends" Puppet Role Plays

Materials: Camera and film, craft sticks, scissors, tape or glue, magazines or catalogs, cardstock, index cards, resealable plastic bag for storing puppets

Preparation: Take a photo of each child in the group or class (full body rather than headshot), and have doubles printed. You may wish to cut away the background and laminate them. Children can help tape or glue the pictures to craft sticks to make stick puppets. Also make extra puppets (at least one per child) by cutting out pictures from catalogs and magazines of varied children and adults. Card stock can be glued to the back for stiffness.

Directions: Each child should have his or her own puppet, the puppet of a friend or classmate, and at least one of the extra puppets. (Store puppets in a resealable plastic bag when not in use.) Children can rotate playing themselves, their friend, or someone new. Have children practice introducing themselves, asking appropriate questions that engage conversation, and being friendly and polite. You may wish to prompt children by demonstrating a scenario with a child. For each scenario, you may wish to focus on one of the ten skills listed on page 33.

Sample Role Play Ideas:

- At a shopping center, you see someone who looks or dresses very differently from you.
- A group of boys (or girls) are playing together. You want to play, but they say, "This is only for boys (or girls)."
- At school you notice a new child is playing or eating alone or needs help with something.
- You are invited to eat at a friend's home. The foods and way of eating are different from what you're used to.

"Parts of a Group" Card Game

Materials: Magazines, markers, scissors, glue, index cards

Preparation: Cut out or draw sets of pictures (such as below) and glue each picture to a separate index card:

Group Cards		Part Cards	
trees in a forest	a person	a single tree	an arm or ear
a jazz band or orchestra	an aquarium of fish	a single instrument	a single fish
a flower garden	a completed puzzle	a single flower	a puzzle piece
a car	a basketball team	a steering wheel	a player

Discussion: Set the Part Cards aside. Place the Group Cards facedown and have a child draw a card. Discuss the various different elements that make up the picture. Talk about how each part completes the whole and makes it work better or makes it more beautiful.

Game Directions: Place all cards face down randomly. The first player turns over two cards, seeking a matching Group Card and Part Card. If the cards are not a match, the child turns them back over. Play continues, with everyone trying to remember the location of the cards. When a child finds a match, have the child explain how the single item is important to the group it belongs in. Continue until all cards are matched.

"We're Unique and Beautiful" Bouquet

Materials: Pictures of flowers from books or catalogs, colored construction paper or tissue paper, scissors, glue, crayons or markers, green florist wire or pipe cleaners, clear tape or green florist tape, photo or hand-drawn picture of each child, large vase or decorated can or wastebasket

Discussion: As a follow-up to the "Parts of a Group" Card Game, discuss various types of flowers, inviting children to talk about which are their favorites and why they like them. Share pictures and descriptions of flowers. Talk about the qualities of each one and about how flowers complement one another when they're together in a bouquet or garden. Relate the discussion to the children by talking about ways that each child adds something to the group; together, the unique individuals make a special group.

Directions: Ask each child to make a favorite type of flower. Help children to cut and fold their chosen flowers from construction or tissue paper and tape or twist green wire for stems. Have each child glue his or her own photograph or hand-drawn self-portrait on a flower petal or center. Display the flowers together in a container.

Variations: Make a "We're Unique and Beautiful" bulletin board display or a poster of flowers, snowflakes, or handprints.

Free Spirit's Learning to Get Along® Series

Help children learn, understand, and practice basic social and emotional skills. Real-life situations, diversity, and concrete examples make these read-aloud books appropriate for childcare settings, schools, and the home. *Each book: 40 pp., color illust., S/C, 9" x 9", ages 4–8.*

ACCEPT AND VALUE EACH PERSON
Introduces diversity and related concepts: respecting differences, being inclusive, and appreciating people just the way they are.

BE CAREFUL AND STAY SAFE
Teaches children how to avoid potential dangers, ask for help, follow directions, use things carefully, and plan ahead.

BE HONEST AND TELL THE TRUTH
Children learn that being honest in words and actions builds self-confidence and trust, and that telling the truth can take courage and tact.

BE POLITE AND KIND
Introduces children to good manners and gracious behavior including saying "Please," "Thank you," "Excuse me," and "I'm sorry."

COOL DOWN AND WORK THROUGH ANGER
Teaches skills for working through anger: self-calming, getting help, talking and listening, apologizing, and viewing others positively.

JOIN IN AND PLAY
Teaches the basics of cooperation, getting along, making friends, and being a friend.

KNOW AND FOLLOW RULES
Shows children that following rules can help us stay safe, learn, be fair, get along, and instill a positive sense of pride.

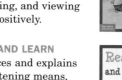

LISTEN AND LEARN
Introduces and explains what listening means, why it's important to listen, and how to listen well.

REACH OUT AND GIVE
Begins with the concept of gratitude; shows children contributing to their community in simple yet meaningful ways.

RESPECT AND TAKE CARE OF THINGS
Children learn to put things where they belong and ask permission to use things. Teaches simple environmental awareness.

SHARE AND TAKE TURNS
Gives reasons to share; describes four ways to share; points out that children can also share their knowledge, creativity, and time.

TALK AND WORK IT OUT
Peaceful conflict resolution is simplified so children can learn to calm down, state the problem, listen, and think of and try solutions.

TRY AND STICK WITH IT
Introduces children to flexibility, stick-to-it-iveness (perseverance), and the benefits of trying something new.

UNDERSTAND AND CARE
Builds empathy in children; guides them to show they care by listening to others and respecting their feelings.

WHEN I FEEL AFRAID
Helps children understand their fears; teaches simple coping skills; encourages children to talk with trusted adults about their fears.

LEARNING TO GET ALONG® SERIES INTERACTIVE SOFTWARE
Children follow along or read on their own, using a special highlight feature to click or hear word definitions. User's Guide included. *For Mac and Windows.*

www.freespirit.com • 800.735.7323

Volume discounts: edsales@freespirit.com
Speakers bureau: speakers@freespirit.com